picture the past

Art ideas to recreate history for children aged five to eleven

Joan Chambers and Molly Hood

Illustrations by Heather Hacking

First published in 1992 by
BELAIR PUBLICATIONS LIMITED
P.O. Box 12, Twickenham, England, TWI 2QL

© 1992 Joan Chambers and Molly Hood
Series Editor Robyn Gordon
Designed by Richard Souper
Photography by Kelvin Freeman
Typesetting by Belair
Printed and Bound by Heanor Gate Printing Limited
ISBN 0 947882 22 7

Acknowledgements

The authors and publishers would like to thank the children and staff of Auriol Middle School, West Ewell, Surrey, and the children and staff of St. Clement's R.C. First School, West Ewell, for their co-operation in making this book, and Alexandra Chambers for the cover artwork.

They would also like to thank the following for their special contribution to the artwork:- Lauren Bennett, Emma Bulbeck, Alexandra Chambers, Tracey Floyd, Katherine Giles and Sheba Khan.

Thanks to Ann Treseder, Paul Stevens and Rebecca Pryor for artefacts, and Michael Peake for his invaluable assistance.

Courtiers carrying Queen Elizabeth I in her litter (see page 42)

Contents

Introduction

Picture the Past provides suggestions for art ideas based on historical themes. All the work illustrated was done by children in the 5-11 age range.

● It is not intended to be a history book although historical information accompanies many of the art ideas. These can used as a starting point or follow-up to a series of history lessons on the periods covered.

● Although the art ideas are based on historical themes, many of them could be included in other topics, or enjoyed as general creative artwork.

● Many of the art ideas can be used across the age range, adapting the techniques to suit each group of children.

● The instructions are written in simple and clear language so that children in the older age range can use the book by themselves, either individually or in groups, to produce their own board displays.

● In addition to the basic materials found in most school stock cupboards, we feel it is very worthwhile having some silver and gold pens and strong black marker pens.

● All the line drawings in this book may be photocopied. Use of the enlarging and reducing facility will enable them to be used in a variety of ways in the classroom.

● Choosing colours selectively is an important factor in creating the visual impression of a period of history. Where papers in the appropriate colours are not available they can be painted beforehand.

● We hope you find this book enjoyable and helpful in providing a source of inspiration for ideas based on the past.

Joan Chambers and Molly Hood

Egyptian

Pleasure Garden

Many wealthy families in Ancient Egypt had a pool in their garden, filled with fish and lotus flowers. It often had attractive plants round the edge to make a border. In such a hot climate it was a pleasant place to relax.

Materials
Pale green for background (or white paper covered with pale green tissue paper)
Smaller piece of turquoise paper for the pool
Scraps of coloured paper
White paper for fish, birds and flowers
Felt-tip pens
Scissors and glue

Draw, colour and cut out fish, birds and flowers. Glue them on to the pool. Glue the pool on to the background to create a border. Decorate the border with shrubs and plants made with felt-tip pens and coloured paper scraps. Mount on contrasting blue or green if required.

● Design a modern pleasure garden around a pool of water. What could it have around it?

● Create a 3D miniature pleasure garden using sand, water, plants, cardboard palm trees etc. on a tray or in a box.

● Make a table display of the various foods that ancient Egyptians would have grown, which are available today. If possible, use pottery dishes and fill with figs, pomegranates, grapes, dates and garlic. Copy pictures of plants from tomb paintings found in books or postcards, and add these drawings to the display.

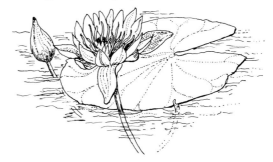

Egyptian

Tomb picture

In this picture of a tomb painting, the scribe Nebamun is hunting wildfowl in the marshes from a papyrus raft and is using a cat to retrieve the birds. He is surrounded by papyrus reeds and grasses and is using a wooden throw stick to hunt.

Find a picture or postcard of a tomb painting and use the following techniques to make it.

Materials
Yellow or gold paper for background
Thin paper for rubbing
Card to make subjects for rubbing
Brown paper for mounting the cut-out pieces
Piece of white paper pleated to make a skirt
Crayons with wrappers removed, in greens, blues and browns
Thin felt-tip pens in dark colours

1. Draw and cut out the components of the picture from the card, e.g. figures, boat, fish, birds, cat, papyrus reeds and water.

2. Place the thin paper over the cardboard shapes and rub with the side of a crayon. Using the same shape, repeat as often as required to make several rows of papyrus reeds.

3. Cut out the rubbings and glue on to brown paper. Cut round these, leaving an edge, and glue on to the background.

4. Glue the skirt on to the figure and decorate the whole picture with felt-tip pens.

● Use this repeated rubbing idea to make a classroom frieze, e.g. soldiers in a battle, or figures in a procession.

Writing folders

For inscriptions on monuments, ancient Egyptians used hieroglyphics which were a combination of signs and pictures. For everyday use, simplified forms were developed. Hieroglyphics were a mystery until the discovery of the Rosetta Stone in l799. This was a slab of basalt showing the same text in Greek, demotic and hieroglyphics. It was the key to understanding the ancient Egyptian script. The names of kings and queens were always written in hieroglyphics in an oval-shaped cartouche.

Materials
Yellow and blue paper
Felt-tip pens in blues, greens and gold
White paper for the cartouche shapes
Scissors and glue

Using one of the coloured papers, fold the outer edges to meet together at the centre. Open out and glue down half a sheet of the other colour on the inside. Cut the top in a symmetrical shape. Cut out cartouche shapes and write and draw about hieroglyphics. Glue these on to the centre of the folder. Decorate the cover with Egyptian patterns using felt-tip pens.

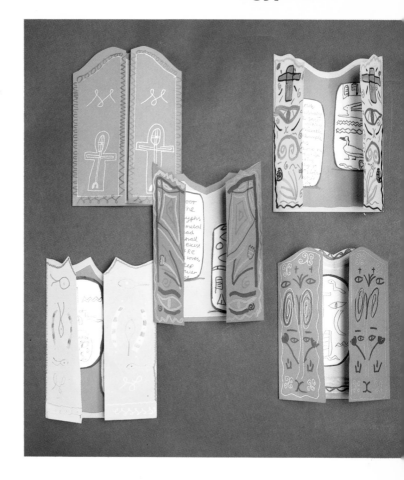

Ankh Abstract

Materials
White paper for background
Tissue paper in oranges and yellows, cut into wavy strips
Plain and corrugated cardboard
Royal blue paint, yellow paint
Paintbrush
Scissors and glue

l. Spread glue all over the white paper and overlap the tissue strips to cover the background.
2. Paint the corrugated cardboard with yellow paint. Leave to dry.
3. Cut the corrugated cardboard into triangles and ankhs (see Tutenkhamen's Wall Tiles). Paint the ridges with blue paint.
4. Glue shapes on to the back ground.
5. Fold a strip of card into a triangle shape, dip in the blue paint and print in the spaces.

Egyptian

Faience Picture

Faience was a type of glazed earthenware in distinctive shades of green and blue. It was made from powdered quartz which was heated in a mould to produce objects such as wine jars and drinking cups. The lotus-flower cups were used for beer, wine and water. Other objects made from this material included ceremonial throwsticks and sacred animals.

Materials
A sheet of white paper for the lotus cup template
Turquoise card
Strips of tissue paper in various shades of green and blue
Felt-tip pens in greens, blues and gold
Scissors and glue

1. Fold the white paper down the middle and draw half a lotus cup shape (see diagram).
2. Cut along the line through both thicknesses and open out.
3. Using this as a template, draw and cut out a cup shape from the blue card.
4. Fold several strips of tissue paper together in half, and half again, and cut a pointed pattern along one edge.
5. Glue the strips on to the cup shapes leaving some spaces in between. When dry, decorate with felt-tip pens.

● Find pictures of other faience objects, e.g. hippopotami, scarabs, cats, and then make them with tissue paper in various shades of blue and green.
● Make Egyptian animals from Plasticine or clay, and paint with thick turquoise paint.
● Cut out animal shapes from card and add details, then place under thin paper and rub over with crayons in blues and greens.

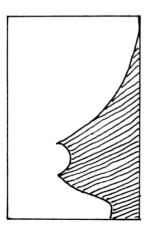

Papyrus Boat Scene

Papyrus reeds were plentiful along the Nile and were used to make paper. The earliest boats were made by lashing the reeds together with twine. The Ancient Egyptians placed tiny model boats in the tombs to provide transport in the next life. Most people lived on the banks of the Nile because the rest of the country was desert, and was considered to be dangerous and inhospitable.

Materials
Blue card for the folded background
Green and brown paper for palm trees, reeds, plants and houses
Corrugated cardboard triangles painted yellow
Yellow paper for sand
Art straws for boat, cut to suitable length
Piece of string
Thin green paint
Felt-tip pens
Scissors and glue

Twist several art straws together and tie with string at each end to make the boat. Cut a wavy line across the yellow paper and separate to form the river. Glue it down on the lower half of the background. Fold the upper half to make a backdrop and prop it up on a table against a wall. Make into a river scene by adding the pyramids, palm trees, reeds and mud brick houses. Place the boat on the river. Make a sail if desired and complete the scene with coloured paper

● Draw and cut out small cardboard figures of ancient Egyptian workers along the Nile performing various tasks, e.g. driving cattle; counting the cattle; operating a shadoof to raise water from the river for irrigation; catching birds and fish; making mud bricks and leaving them to dry in the sun; cutting papyrus reeds. Make the figures stand up. Move them round and tell stories about them.

Egyptian

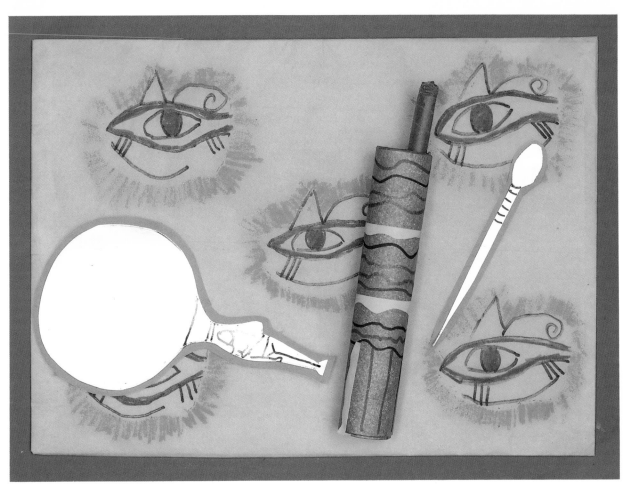

Wedjat Eye

Personal appearance was very important to the Ancient Egyptians. Both men and women liked to wear eye make-up. Green eye paint was made from malachite, and black eye paint (or 'kohl') was made from lead ore. The minerals were mixed with water and kept in containers (like the one in the photograph above) which were often carved and decorated.

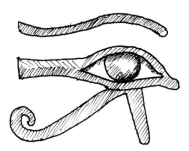

The wedjat eye was a protective symbol and represented the lunar eye of the god of light and was therefore a popular amulet, or charm. It was often used as a protection against evil and so it frequently appeared in tomb and coffin decorations and on funerary jewellery.

Materials

Piece of paper for background
Gold or yellow tissue paper larger than background
Small piece of card to make the eye
Piece of gold card
Cardboard roll covered in turquoise tissue paper and decorated
Old pencil covered in tissue paper
Pastels, felt-tip pens
Scissors and glue

1. Cover the background paper with the tissue paper and glue the edges down at the back.
2. Draw and cut out a wedjat eye from the card.
3. Using the eye as a template, rub away from the shape with pastels. Repeat several times.
4. Outline with felt-tip pens where necessary.
5. Glue down the eye paint container and add other objects of adornment, e.g. mirror and hairpins made from the gold card.

● Bring in eye make-up and try to make up your eyes to look like Ancient Egyptians (both boys and girls). Have make-up remover ready.
● Design a modern good luck charm based on a drawing of an eye.

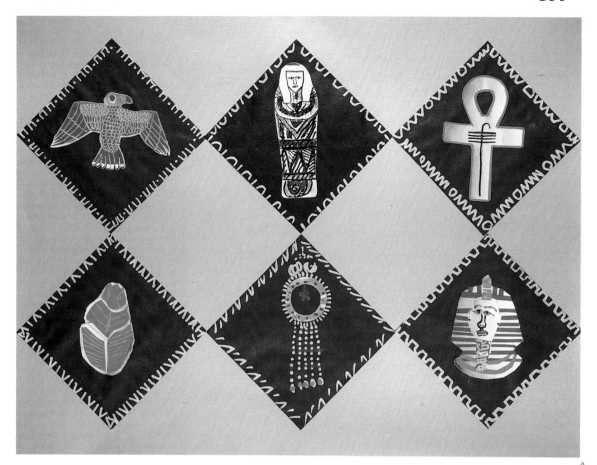

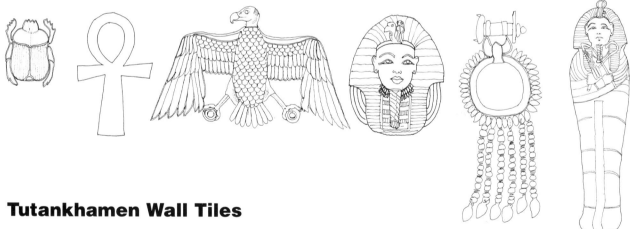

Tutankhamen Wall Tiles

This is a quick and easy way to display the treasures of Tutankhamen's tomb, e.g. vulture, coffin, ankh (key of life), scarab, earring and mask.

Materials
Squares of black paper
Pieces of coloured gummed paper
Gold pen and felt-tip pens
Ruler
Scissors

Find pictures of objects connected with Tutankhamen. Draw these on the back of the gummed paper, cut out and glue on to the middle of the square. Place a ruler a little way in from the edge of the square. Keeping the ruler firmly in place with one hand, draw simple patterns with gold pen, moving between the ruler and the edge of the paper. This creates a straight border without drawing a line.

● Glue the tiles back to back, with a piece of cardboard in between and hang from a corner to make mobiles.

● These could be alternated with pieces of writing and displayed in a single layer around the classroom to form a long frieze.

Egyptian

The Pharaoh's Coffin

The mummy of Tutankhamen was placed in a series of three coffins. The coffin containing the mummy was made of gold; the second was made of gold-plated wood and inlaid with coloured glass and stones (see photograph); the outer coffin was also carved from wood and overlaid with gold foil.

Materials
White and royal blue paper
Art straws painted gold and royal blue
Gold paint or gold felt-tip pen
Pastels in blue, red and yellow

1. Draw one of the inner coffins from Tutankhamen's tomb on the white paper.
2. Decorate the body section with pastel in rows of colour.
3. Paint the face and hands gold. Cut out a beard and glue down.
4. Glue down straws to make headdress, crook and flail. Add dabs of blue to the crook and flail. Glue some straws to the front of the body.
5. Glue on to royal blue paper and mount on gold if desired.

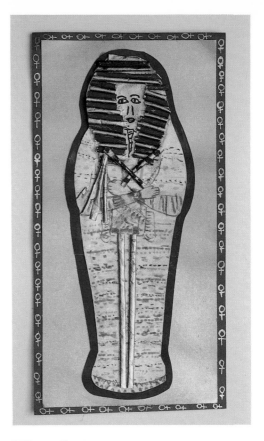

The Cat

Bastet, the cat goddess, was believed to have the power to help crops grow. Cats were greatly loved and revered in Ancient Egypt. Many hundreds of mummified cats have been discovered near the temple of Bastet in the northern Egyptian town where she was especially worshipped. They are wrapped with extremely neat and decorative bindings. Other sacred animals were mummified too, such as ibises and baboons.

Materials
Two layers of stiff black paper or thin card
Gold paper for background
White paper to mount the picture
Small scraps of silver paper
Silver pen or white pencil
Pencil and felt-tip pens
Scissors and glue

Draw a simple outline of a cat on the top layer of black paper. Hold both layers of paper together and cut out two identical cat shapes. Draw the face and front legs on the top shape only. Cut round this and glue on to the bottom layer. Glue the cat on to the background, add jewellery and glue a small piece of card under the front legs to make them stand out. Outline the front legs and add features with silver pen.

Make a border of hieroglyphics using felt-tip pens.

Throne and Fans

Tutankhamen's throne was made of wood and carved with animals' heads and feet. It was covered with gold and silver leaf and decorated with semi-precious stones and coloured glass. The picture on the throne is of the young Tutankhamen and his wife (see illustration on page 4).

Make a throne from scrapbox materials either copied from a picture of Tutankhamen's throne or based on your own design.

Fans

Some Egyptian fans had long handles, were a distinctive semi-circular shape and made with ostrich feathers. A fan found in Tutankhamen's tomb was made of gold, and embossed with a hunting scene.

Materials
White cardboard
White tissue paper
Straws (or wooden garden sticks) covered with blue tissue paper for handles
Felt-tip pens in blues, greens, yellows and gold
Scissors and glue

1. Draw and cut out a semi-circle from the white card and decorate with felt-tip pens using Egyptian motifs.
2. Cut a double strip of white tissue paper, fringe it along one edge and glue it around the semi-circular shape to make the feathers.
3. Glue straws on to the back of the fan.

On a larger scale, decorate a classroom chair as a throne and make lifesize fans. Use these for drama activities.

Lotus Flower Border

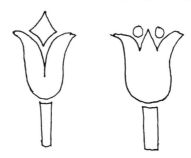

Draw and cut out the two shapes above. Glue on details and, when dry, place the shapes under a strip of thin paper and rub over with crayons in blue and green to create the border.

Egyptian

Egyptian Jewellery

Egyptian jewellery was made of gold and semi-precious stones such as red carnelian, blue lapis lazuli and turquoise. Diamonds, rubies and emeralds were not used because Ancient Egyptians did not know of their existence. Silver was rarely used, and at that time was more precious than gold.

Rolled Paper Jewellery

Blue card for background, black card for mount
Strips of gold paper, and red, blue and black paper
Brown paper for heads and arms, black paper for hair

ARMS AND HANDS: Children draw around their own forearm and hand on brown paper and cut out the shape. Roll up strips and glue down to form beads. Decorate the arms and hands with bracelets and rings made from paper beads.

HEADS: Draw a profile of head and shoulders on brown paper. Sit the profile on black paper and draw a wig. Make a slit in the wig and fit it over the head. Decorate with necklaces, earrings etc. Add left-over strips to the black card to make the mount.

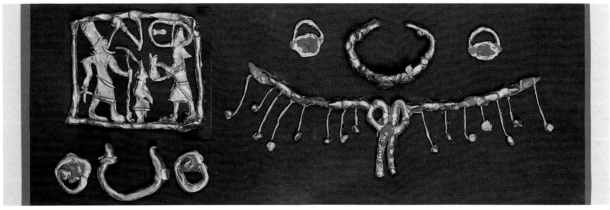

Plasticine Jewellery

Form Plasticine into necklaces, bracelets, rings etc. Add beads in Egyptian colours made with red, blue and brown Plasticine (or Plasticine painted these colours to imitate gemstones). Paint with gold paint, applied thickly. Leave to dry and mount on black card.

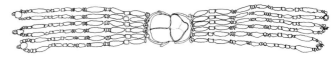

This is a useful way of using old Plasticine, but make sure that the paint is mixed thickly enough to cover it. Younger children could make pasta shapes in these colours.

Vases

These pots, although beautifully decorated, were not ornaments. They were made to last and withstand constant daily use. Black-figure ware had black figures painted on a red background, which was the natural colour of the clay. They were decorated with scenes from real life and mythology.

Materials
Paper for template
Black paper
Red and orange tissue paper
Strong black marker pen
Scissors and glue

1. Fold the paper in half and draw half a pot, making sure to start drawing at the fold so that it opens out in the correct way. Cut along the line, through both thicknesses, and open out as a template.

2. Draw around the template on the black paper and cut out the shape. Fold this in half and cut out some simple shapes starting at the fold.
3. On the back of the pot, glue down a layer of red and a layer of orange tissue paper to cover the spaces.
4. Turn over and decorate with black paper shapes and marker pens. Place on a window to make a display.

● Experiment with other ways to make black-figure ware, e.g. crayons or paint.

● Use terracotta clay or Plasticine to make small pots and decorate them with thick black paint applied with a small brush.

Greek

Greek Display

Cut a large piece of white paper into hills for the background shape. Paint some corrugated cardboard white. When dry, cut into strips of different lengths to make a temple shape with steps at the front. Cut some smaller pieces to represent broken columns.

Find pictures of Greek pottery and make plate designs on red circles with black marker pens. Mount on white circles and edge with black pen.

Make a statue of a goddess to stand in the temple. Cut out old coin shapes from silver card and decorate with gold and black pens.

Use this display as a background for written work or drawings. Add pictures of Greek temples cut from travel magazines and brochures.

This could be made on a larger scale to represent a temple. Use eight columns to make the front of the Parthenon in Athens. Display pieces of work in the spaces between the columns.

Corinthian

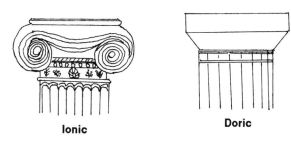

Ionic

Doric

These are three different capital designs

16

Dolphin Fresco

Fragments of this fresco, or wall painting, were found at the palace of Knossos in Crete. These pieces were then incorporated into an artist's impression of the original. Minoan painters used colours believed to be lucky, e.g. red and sky blue. The frescoes were made by painting the walls while the plaster was still wet.

Materials
Blue card or paper for dolphins
Black paper for coral, orange paper for fish
White or beige paper for background
Black, blue and orange paint
Thin paintbrush
Crayons in blues and greens (with wrappers removed)
Small piece of card for motif
Thin paper for rubbing motif
Coloured paper for mounting picture and motifs
Black felt-tip pen
Scissors and glue

1. Using thin blue paint, make sea patterns on the background.
2. Draw and cut out one dolphin from the blue card. Use this as a template to make four more dolphins.

3. Paint an orange stripe on three dolphins facing in one direction, the other two facing the opposite way.
4. Make small fish from the orange paper. Glue these and the dolphins on to the background.
5. Cut out coral from the black paper and glue along the top and bottom of the picture. Use black paint round the edge of the coral.
6. Decorate with felt-tip pens.

To make motif
Cut a circular rosette shape from the card. Glue thin strips of card across it. Leave to dry, cover with thin paper and rub over with the side of a crayon. Repeat to make border pattern. Cut out the motifs and glue round the picture on the coloured mounting paper.

● Draw and colour another fresco, e.g. bulldancing. Cut into six or eight pieces. Remove two or three of the pieces and glue the rest on to a background. Swap with a partner and try to complete the picture.

Greek

Trireme

A trireme was a light, fast warship. It had three banks of oars, hence its name. As there was very little room for living quarters, soldiers only went to sea for a short time. It had a linen sail fastened to the mast with leather thongs. The sail and the mast were laid on the deck during battle. On the front was a bronze spike used for ramming the enemy ships. An eye was painted on the front.

Materials

Blue card for background
Thin card, painted brown, for trireme
Art straws painted brown
Wavy strips of blue paper for the sea
Pale blue paper and red paper strips for the sail (or paint stripes on the blue)
Paint in various colours, thin paintbrush
Scissors and glue

1. Draw and cut out a trireme shape from the brown card.
2. Paint details on the trireme.
3. Glue down straws to make planks and oars.
4. Make a blue sail and add red paper strips. Glue it on to a straw mast.

5. Glue the trireme on the background at its base. Make it stand out at the top by gluing a small piece of card behind.
6. Fold the wavy sea strips in half lengthwise and make them stand up by gluing the lower half only.

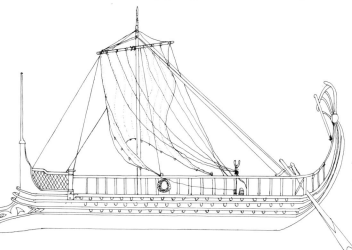

● Create a sea battle by making a large display with several triremes and adding Greek figures.
● Make a collection of words which begin with 'tri', e.g. triangle, tripod, tricycle, trident. Illustrate them.

Greek Armour

In ancient Athens, all men had to do two years Army service. After one year the State gave them a sword and a shield. Other armour such as breastplates had to be bought out of their own money. Hoplites, or foot-soldiers, fought with lances and double-edged swords. They used round shields and shinguards made of bronze or leather. The bronze helmets had horse-hair crests to make the soldiers look taller.

Materials
Beige paper for mounting
Black and red squares of paper
Gold foil
Black paper
Black marker pen
Scissors and glue

Draw examples of Greek armour on the back of a piece of gold paper. Cut them out and glue one on to each square. Decorate with black pen and paper. Glue on to the background and add spears to complete the picture.

● Find out about a modern Infantry soldier and list the differences in clothing and weapons.

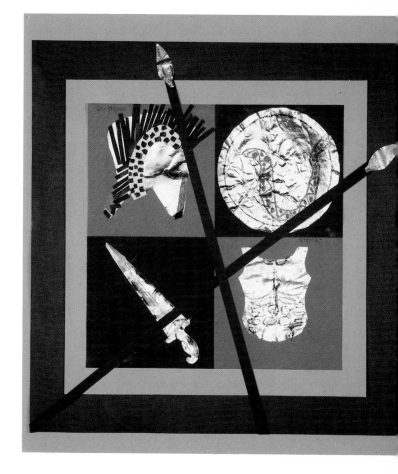

This is a replica of the original disc of Phaistos

Disc of Phaistos

This terracotta disc was found in the Palace of Phaistos on the island of Crete. The forty-five different symbols were pressed into the clay while it was still wet. Despite investigation by many experts, no-one has been able to decipher the code with any certainty.

● Draw the table of symbols and try to decode them in your own way.

● Make a disc using brown cardboard and white string for the spiral. Paint the symbols on with white paint on both sides. Make into a mobile.

● Use Plasticine to make a disc. Press a sharp instrument into the surface to make the symbols and paint them white.

Greek

Trojan Horse

1. Print some sheets of coloured paper with thick paint and various objects such as crumpled paper, cotton wool, plastic construction bricks, thick cardboard strips, rulers, sponges.

2. When dry, cut these up to make a picture. Glue on to a printed background. Make a door which opens in the Trojan horse and add a ladder and soldiers.

Greek Temples

Copy this pediment shape on to a large sheet of paper, add columns either side and use the space for creative writing.

Greeks built large beautiful temples to house the statues of their gods. At the front were columns (6, 8, or sometimes I0) supporting a large triangular pediment. The tops of Greek columns were called capitals. There were three types (see page I6).

The statues in the pediment usually represented a story from Greek mythology showing groups of gods, or heroes in battle.

● Draw your own figures in the pediment. Choose poses (sitting, kneeling, lying down) which fit into the triangular shape. The background should be coloured blue, and the eyes and mouths and some of the clothes coloured in blue and red. Weapons and metal objects were added to the statues. Use a gold pen to draw these.

● Write your own poem or story about the Greek gods and heroes. Use the picture in the pediment to illustrate it.

● Design your own buildings using Greek columns and pediments as decoration.

Myths and Legends - Midas and Icarus

Greek children were told wonderful stories about the heroes and heroines of ancient Greece. The gods and goddesses often appeared in these adventures. The myths and legends are particularly suitable for creative artwork as there are many stories open to interpretation. Much of our knowledge of these has come from ancient poems and stories.

Materials
A circle of black paper
White paper for background
Tissue paper, foil and coloured paper
Coloured paper for mount
Felt-tip pens
Scissors and glue

Use the materials above to create a collage picture which tells the story of a legend. Mount on to coloured paper and then on a square of white to make a border. Decorate the edge with a Greek key pattern in felt-tip pens.

● Written work about the legend can be glued on to the bottom of the picture.

● Create a story sequence on smaller circles, highlighting the main parts of the story.

● Make up mimes connected with famous myths and legends. Let the rest of the group guess which ones they are.

● Some suitable myths and legends are: Persephone, Atlanta, Theseus and the Minotaur, Pegasus.

● Write and draw about 'compound' monsters from Greek mythology, e.g. woman/bird - harpies
man/bull - minotaur
man/horse - centaur

Invent your own compound monster.

Roman

Pompeian Room

In Roman times, walls were often painted in bright colours to imitate marble and wood panelling. The candelabra design (as on the red panels in the photograph) was very popular. The large panel at the top often had plants, animals and figures painted on it. Pompeian houses were sparsely furnished, the most important furniture being the couches found in the dining room.

Materials

Coloured paper for background, e.g. brown
Paper or thin card in appropriate colours, e.g. blue, pale green, dull yellow, dark red
Gold pen or gold paint
Crayons, with wrappers removed, in brown, green, blue and black
White paper for figures
Paper for furniture
Adhesive tape
Felt-tip pens
Scissors and glue

1. Cut out straight pieces from the thin card, e.g. squares, rectangles. (A trimmer is very useful for this.)

2. Crease strips of adhesive tape on to a small piece of paper to create a rough surface.

3. To create a marbled effect, place the pieces of coloured card over this and rub with the side of a crayon using the colours above.

4. Mount some pieces on a contrasting colour, e.g. red on pale green. Trim and glue on to the background leaving spaces in between where appropriate.

5. Decorate the wall panels with gold pen. Glue down the furniture and figures.

● Working in pairs, draw some fragments of a wall design. Swap designs and try to complete them.

● Create a Roman room using a box. Add a mosaic floor and make pieces of furniture.

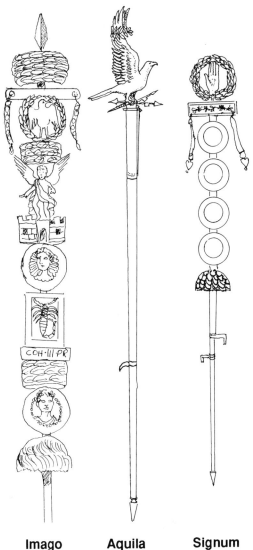

Imago   Aquila   Signum

Shield and Standard

The wooden shields were rectangular and covered in leather and linen. They were decorated with bronze and painted designs. There were three main types of standard. The 'aquila' (eagle) was the standard for the entire legion and it was usually made of silver and gold. The 'signa' was the standard for each century (l00 men). The 'imago' carried the Emperor's portrait. They were carried on poles when marching, then stuck into the ground when the soldiers made camp.

Materials

Silver and gold card (or card covered with gold and silver paper)
Blue or red card, or card covered with blue or red tissue, for shield
Strip of brown card for each standard
Piece of white paper for shield motif
Black paper for background
Scraps of red for streamers
Gold and black marker pens
Scissors and glue

1. Cut out the motif for the shield from white paper. Glue on to a shield shape and decorate with black and gold pens.
2. Using the silver and gold card, cut out circles and rectangles and glue on to the strip of card. Decorate with felt-tip pens and add scraps to make streamers.

● Design a portrait of an emperor for the top of a standard.

● Cardboard rolls cut in half lengthwise give curved shapes for small shields. Arrange these to make a 'tortoise' formation.

● Make up Latin names. Have a 'Roman day' and put these names in a hat. Choose one and use it for a day. Create a Roman area with chairs made into couches and covered with material. Dress up in togas made from sheets. Eat Roman food, e.g. grapes, figs, round loaves of bread. Make a candle clock and a sundial.

Roman

A Gorgon's Head

Gorgons were terrifying creatures from Greek and Roman mythology. This is the head of a male Gorgon but the female Medusa and her sisters are better known - particularly as they had live snakes for hair and the sight of them turned people to stone. Perseus was able to slay Medusa because he observed her, indirectly, in the reflection in his highly polished shield. He gave her head to the goddess Minerva who wore it on her breastplate and thereafter retained Gorgons as one of her special symbols. This stone Gorgon head is from the temple of Minerva in Bath.

Materials
Thin stone-coloured paper (beige or grey)
Scraps of cardboard
Crayons, with wrappers removed, in brown, orange and black
Paper for background
Scissors and glue

1. Cut a circle from the cardboard. Cut a smaller circle and glue it in the centre for a face. Add features and hair cut from card. Leave it to dry.
2. Place the thin paper over the face and, using the side of a crayon, rub firmly over the face. Use different colours to get a shaded effect.

Lararium

Every Roman home had a lararium. This was a shrine to the household gods. It was usually placed in the *atrium* (entrance hall) or set into the wall.

Materials
White paper for background
Corrugated cardboard
Coloured paper for marble stand
Adhesive tape
Pastels, crayons, pencil
Scissors and glue

1. Draw a lararium with a pencil on the white paper.
2. Cut pieces of corrugated cardboard to make the outside shape.
3. Cut a piece of coloured cardboard to make the stand. Marble it by rubbing over creased adhesive tape (as in Pompeian Room artwork on page 22). Glue it on to the paper underneath the corrugated card.
4. Decorate with pastels, smudging them for a soft effect. Find out about various Roman Gods. Design a special shrine to one of them.

3. Cut round the rubbing and glue on to a background. Use this technique to create the look of other stone sculptures.

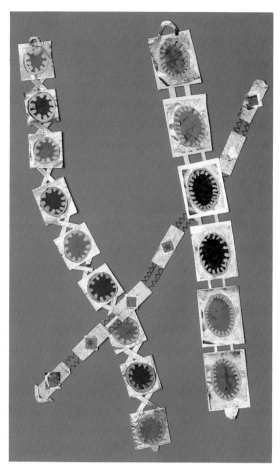

Roman Bracelets

Most Roman jewellery was made of gold and was often decorated with metal fretwork. The patterns were chiselled from sheets of gold, and attractive semi-precious stones were set into it. Later on, stones such as emeralds became very popular.

Materials
A selection of different types of gold paper card
Paper in colours of semi-precious stones, e.g. dark red, blue, black
Gold pen
Crayons in dark colours, with wrappers removed
Adhesive tape and paper
Scissors and glue

1. To create a textured effect, rub with the side of a crayon on the coloured paper placed over the creased adhesive tape. (See Pompeian room - Steps 2 and 3, page 22.)
2. Cut this into oval shapes to make gemstones.
3. Cut the gold paper or card into rectangles and decorate with the gold papers and gemstones.
4. Draw details in gold pen and cut and glue on fasteners.
5. Glue several bracelets on to a coloured background for display.

● Design a museum case, make some ancient jewellery for it and label the 'exhibits'. Write about
   - how the jewellery was discovered
   - the condition it was in
   - who the owners might have been.

Roman Portrait

In Roman houses, portraits of the occupants were sometimes painted on the plaster wall. This girl is holding a wax tablet and a stylus for writing. One end of the stylus was flat to get rid of mistakes and smooth the tablet over. The original portrait was painted on a wall in Pompeii.

Materials
A circle of beige or white paper crushed and flattened out, then washed over with cold tea
Piece of crumpled paper
Thin paints in soft colours, paintbrush
Coloured pencil and crayons, without wrappers, in brown
Paper for mount
Pencil
Scissors and glue

1. Find a picture of an ancient Roman. Copy it in pencil on to the circle and paint it. Leave to dry.
2. Dab the portrait with crumpled paper dipped in paint. When dry, rub softly with the side of a crayon.

● Use this technique for ageing other things, e.g. scrolls.

Roman

Mosaics

Many Roman villas had beautiful mosaic floors. The square tiles were made of pieces of clay, stone and coloured glass which were pressed into wet plaster. Some had geometric designs and others had pictures of animals, plants and people.

Materials
Thin white paper which has been washed over with pale earth colours, e.g. beige, brown, green, dull red
Black paper for background
Ruler, pencil
Scissors and glue

1. Cut the coloured paper into thin strips and keep some for the border. Place a few strips on top of each other and cut into small squares. Keep the coloured squares in separate containers.
2. Rule a line around the edge of the paper to make a border.
3. Draw a simple mosaic picture outline on the black paper, e.g. volcano, dolphin, ship, tree.
4. Spread glue on a small area and cover with the squares, spaced slightly apart. Repeat in small sections.
5. Glue the thin strips of paper over the ruled lines to make a border.

● Design a motif suitable for a dining room or bathroom (e.g. vegetables, fruit, or underwater creatures).

● Roll out Plasticine into a flat square. Press small pebbles and stones of different colours into the surface to make a mosaic pattern.

● This could be done on a much larger scale to make a   classroom mosaic.

Amphorae

Amphorae were pottery containers with handles at the side and a pointed base. They held wine and oil and were used for transporting these products by sea to other countries. Many have survived intact beneath the sea in ancient shipwrecks.

Materials
White paper for background
Thin paint washes in blues and greens (add extra water to the paint to make a wash)
Crayons in brown and white

1. Draw some amphorae and the hull of a wrecked ship on the white paper, pressing heavily with the crayons. Add patterns and underwater details to make a shipwreck picture.
2. Wash over the picture starting at the top of the page and using wavy lines of blue and green paint.

● Write a story about the discovery of a shipwreck.

● Draw a grid picture to show which artefacts were found in each section of the wreck. What other things might be found (e.g. coins, plates, statues)?

● Use two identical terracotta flowerpots. Beforehand, break one into several pieces and bury in a box of sand. Show the other one to the children, let them find the pieces and re-assemble the pot. Write about how they did it and the difficulties involved. Draw the 'jigsaw pot' after the pieces have been glued together.

● Investigate ways of making things look old. What methods could you use to make something look older?

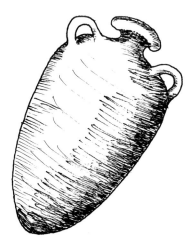

Roman

Aqueduct

In Roman times, aqueducts carried water from the hills to nearby towns. The water travelled in channels supported by huge stone arches.

Materials
Black paper
Tissue paper in blues, greens and white
Black felt-tip pens
Pencil
Scissors and glue

1. Make a frame from the black paper by folding in half and cutting out the middle part, starting at the fold.
2. Glue a double layer of blue tissue on to the frame. Add blue and green waves made from tissue paper.
3. Cut three strips of black paper the width of the picture. Make two strips into bridges of the same height, with the third one (on top) smaller.
4. Fold each strip into six equal parts. Keep the strip folded and draw an archway on the top section. Cut through all the layers at the same time to make six arches when opened out. Glue down to make the three levels of the aqueduct and add details.

● Use this design to make a 3D model which could carry water along the top channel.

Thermal Window

This type of window is known as a thermal window. It was a characteristic feature of Roman public baths.

Use the same technique as above to make a semi-circular window. Glue down two narrow black strips to make divisions. Make a picture connected with the Roman Baths, e.g. a fountain or motifs from the baths.

● Find some pictures of Roman baths and look for other architectural features.

● Design other window shapes, using the same technique, and decide which type of buildings would contain these best, e.g. town hall, cinema, church or modern swimming pool.

28

Tudor and Stuart

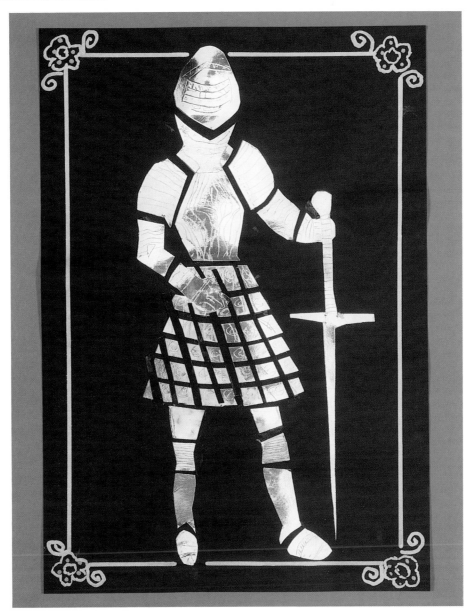

The Armour of Henry VIII

Henry VIII not only enjoyed watching tournaments, he actually participated in jousts himself. Some of the armour he wore for this still survives.

Materials
Black paper for background
Thin black paper strips
Silver card
Pencil
Scissors and glue

1. Look at the line drawings on the following page.
2. Draw a simple outline of an armoured figure on the back of the card and cut this out.
3. Cut the figure into sections. Glue these on to the background leaving spaces between them.

4. Decorate by scoring with scissor points and add black strips to create further decorations.
5. Decorate the edge of the picture with silver paints.

N.B. If silver card is not available, use silver foil or paper glued on to thin card.

● Design some armour for horses.

● Draw Henry's armour at different stages of his life, i.e. as he became fatter.

● Find out what happens at a joust, or tournament. Make a picture from card in which the figures can move.

Tudor and Stuart

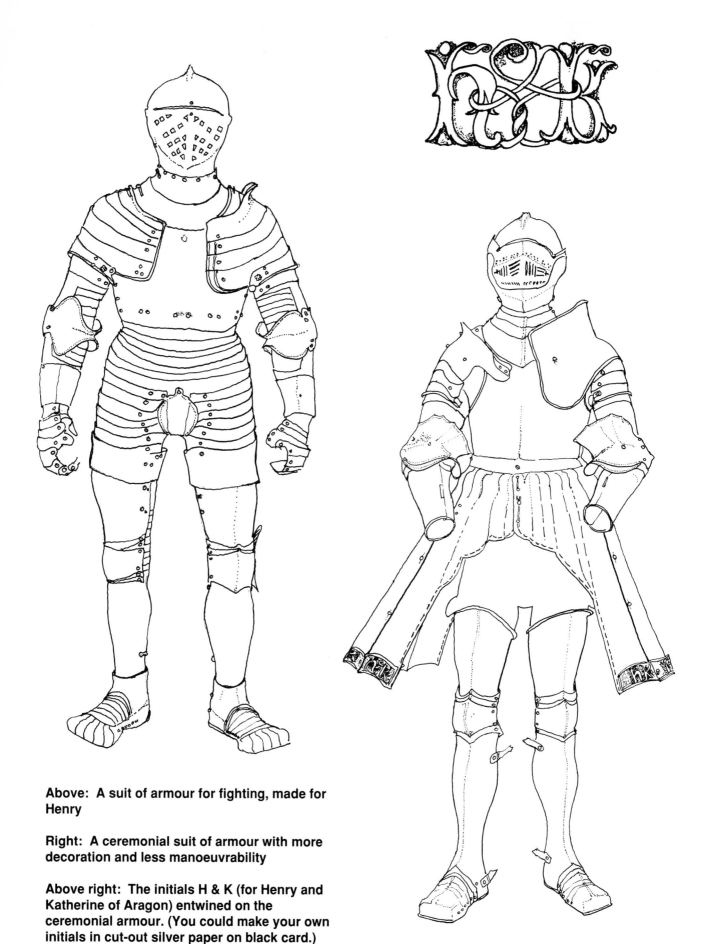

Above: A suit of armour for fighting, made for Henry

Right: A ceremonial suit of armour with more decoration and less manoeuvrability

Above right: The initials H & K (for Henry and Katherine of Aragon) entwined on the ceremonial armour. (You could make your own initials in cut-out silver paper on black card.)

Tudor Portraits

Tudor portraits, to look more authentic, should be mounted on a gold or dark coloured background, e.g. dark red, green, brown or black. The Tudors liked richly patterned fabrics. Gold pen can be used to create this look.

Materials
Collage materials, e.g. fabric, fur fabric, lace, gold trimmings, beads
Strips of card for frames
Coloured card in rich colours for the background
White card for figures
Large sheet of thin brown card or paper
Gold pen
A variety of brown crayons, with the wrappers removed
Felt-tip pens, pencil
Scissors and strong glue

1. Draw a figure on white paper using a pencil.

2. Decorate with collage materials and felt-tip pens.
3. Cut around the figure and glue on to the background.
4. Glue strips around the edge to make a frame. Use gold pens and scraps to complete the portraits and frames.
5. Using the sides of the brown crayons rub over a large sheet of paper placed on a wooden surface, e.g. table, fence, shed.
6. Glue the portraits on to the rubbed background (which gives the impression of a wooden background) and decorate with Tudor roses.

● Create a background with a dark wooden Tudor staircase set at an angle across the page. Place Tudor portraits on the wall above the staircase.

Tudor and Stuart

The Joker

The king's fool, or jester, was the model for the joker on a playing card. Henry VIII's personal jester for many years was Will Somers. Although it was dangerous to offend the king, he, as licensed fool, had special permission to joke and mock without fear of punishment.

Materials
White card for background (to make large playing card)
Gummed paper in two colours, preferably red and green
Felt- tip pens
Scissors and glue

1. Round off the corners of the white card with scissors.
2. Hold the gummed paper together with the coloured sides facing, and draw and cut half an upper body.
3. Turn the remaining gummed papers over - still holding them together and, with the coloured sides still facing, draw and cut out one leg.

4. Turn the paper over again and cut out half a skirt. Assemble the pieces on the background and glue down. Add a hat, collar and shoes, as above.
5. Add hands, and decorate with details in felt-tip pens.

● To make a simpler version, draw and colour a figure as shown in the small line drawing above.

● Design your own packs of cards. Invent some games with them.

● Make up some Tudor jokes (adapt some modern ones by substituting Tudor names).

● Think of some tricks that a monarch's fool might have played to amuse the court. Write or draw them.

● Act out a scene with Henry VIII, his fool and some of his courtiers.

Window Shields

In order to recognise each other in their full armour, knights wore a simple design on their shields and arms. These emblems were unique to the individual. As the number of knights increased, the designs became more complicated to avoid duplication. A lasting record of the shield designs can be found in stained glass windows.

Draw a shield outline on the black paper. Fold in half lengthwise and, starting at the fold, draw a line a little way in from the edge along the four sides. Push the scissors through and cut along the line. Open out and glue it on to two different colours of tissue paper, adding an extra layer of tissue for more intense colour. Add motifs cut from coloured paper and display on a window.

Miniatures

Tudor miniatures were tiny portraits painted on thin vellum glued to playing-cards. Limners (miniature painters) made their own brushes from squirrels' tails, birds' quills and ivory or wooden sticks. These valuable portraits were often kept in beautiful ivory boxes, for protection and safe-keeping, and were the Tudor equivalent of modern photographs. They were easily carried or worn, e.g. as shoe decorations and jewellery.

Materials

Small piece of royal blue paper for background
Black paper for mount, gold paper for frame
Thin white paper
Small template shapes - oval, circle, square
Felt-tip pens, scissors and glue

Draw round a template on the back of the gold paper and cut it out. Fold this in half and cut out an inner shape to make the frame. Glue the gold frame on the blue background and trim round the edge. Place the thin white paper over the gold frame and trace along the inner edge. Cut this out. Within this white shape, draw the head and shoulders and fit into frame shape. Decorate with felt-tip pens. Glue on to black mount.

Tudor and Stuart

Weapon Display

Weapons were often decorated with elaborate patterns. Swords had a curved guard to protect the swordsman's hand. Pikes were very long and made of wood with steel points. Pole-axes were shorter and had blades which were intricately carved.

Materials
Yellow paper for background
Silver and black paper for weapons
Black paper for mounting

1. Cut a symmetrical shape from the yellow paper, making it smaller than the black paper. Glue on to the black background.
2. Draw weapon shapes on the silver paper and cut out details from the black paper, e.g. swords, daggers, spears, shields etc.
3. Arrange in a pattern on the yellow background first, then glue down, making the shield stand out.

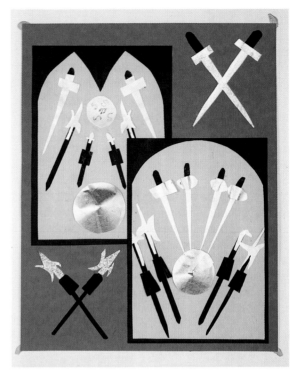

Tudor Lady

Tudor dresses had low square necks, close-fitting waists and heavy full skirts which were often embroidered. The sleeves were wide at the bottom and sometimes trimmed with fur. The outer layer or gown was worn over a kirtle which was a skirt and bodice joined together. The gable hood was often called a kennel. A white coif was worn underneath it, and it was held in place by a piece of jewelled metal.

Materials
Plain paper in dark red, green, gold, black
Wrapping paper with a small pattern in appropriate colours
White paper for figure
Coloured paper for background
Thin card for frame
Felt-tip pens
Scissors and glue

1. Find some pictures of Tudor ladies in costume and draw a figure on the white paper.
2. Decorate the figure with the plain paper and wrapping paper.
3. Draw details in felt-tip pen. Cut out the figure and glue on to background.
4. Cut out a frame from the thin card and cover with wrapping paper.
5. Glue the frame on to background. Use gold and felt-tip pens to decorate the picture.

Nonsuch Palace

Nonsuch Palace (near Cheam, Surrey) has completely disappeared with little remaining record of it. The name was given to describe the outstanding and lavish architecture - 'nonesuch like it'. It was extremely elaborate, even though the site was only the size of a football pitch.

Materials
White paper for background
Blue and green tissue paper larger than background
Stiff paper for the palace
Felt-tips pens
Scissors and glue
1. Glue the tissue on to the background and glue the surplus at the back.
2. Draw and cut out a palace from the stiff paper and glue on to the background.
3. Make towers from the stiff paper by folding rectangles lengthwise into sections and glue in position.
4. Decorate with felt-tip pens.

● Imagine an excavation which unearths a lost Tudor palace. Write about who lived there and why it disappeared.

● Find out about ghost stories from Tudor times. Invent a ghost story for Nonsuch Palace.

● Design your own Tudor Palace.

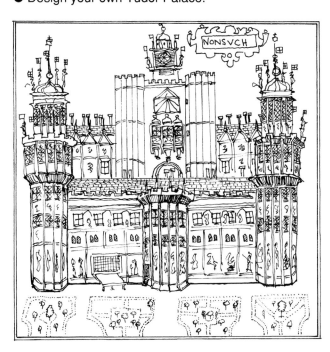

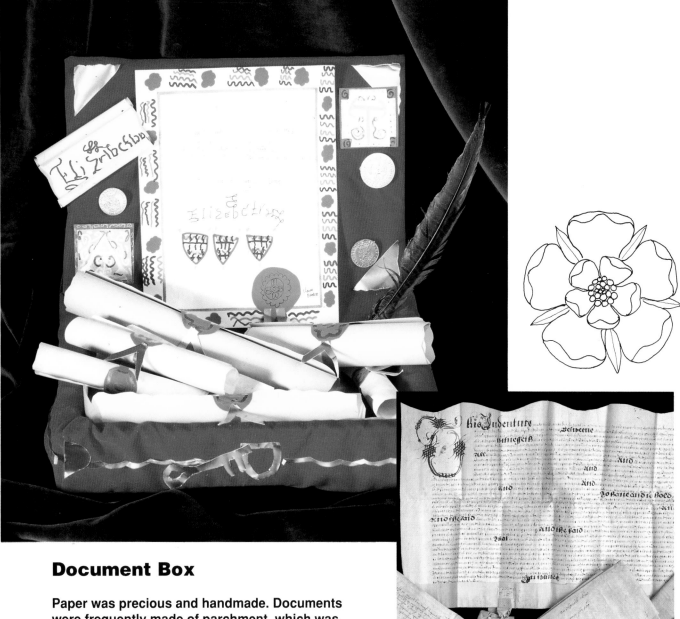

Document Box

Paper was precious and handmade. Documents were frequently made of parchment, which was dried and cleaned animal skin. Vellum was a fine type of parchment made from calves' skin.

The documents shown in the smaller photograph are original documents which were folded, not rolled. The oldest dates back to 1607. The parchment has survived and is in remarkably good condition.

Create the look of old paper or parchment by washing over white paper with a thin yellow-brown paint; or dab with a wet tea-bag or coffee. Leave to dry, then cut a wavy pattern along the edges; or the rolled edges can be burnt (under close supervision) with a match. After the document has been written, make a seal of a Tudor rose from red gummed paper and gold paper. Roll it up and tie with a narrow ribbon.

Some suggestions for contents:
- a request for a queen's or princess's hand in marriage
- a letter of complaint from one king to another
- a peace treaty between countries
- a letter from a traitor begging forgiveness

● Make a document box by painting a cereal box with gold paint and glue on some velvet or brocade as a lining. Decorate with foil shapes and make a lock and key from gold card. Add signatures and drawings of coins. Add a quill feather.

● Write about how documents were made - adding a seal and decorating the border with Tudor motifs.

Tudor Jewellery

Variations on this pendant appear in several Tudor portraits, including one of the young Princess Elizabeth. This cruciform jewellery set with black diamonds and hung with three large pearl drops, was pinned at the neckline of a Tudor gown.

Materials
Gold card
Strips of gold card
Scraps of gold doily, card and black paper
White Plasticine
Broken jewellery
Pieces of plain fabric
Scissors and strong glue

1. Draw a square on the back of the gold card and cut it out.
2. Glue the black scraps on to this to form a cross from corner to corner, and add scraps and broken jewellery.

3. Make the three large 'pearls' from Plasticine and glue on, as shown.
4. Glue on to fabric background and make a frame from the gold strips.

● Make a necklace with an initial letter like Anne Boleyn's 'B', using your own initial, or that of a friend.

A necklace worn by Anne Boleyn

● Design a jewel box as a gift for a queen.

● Design a piece of jewellery using specific materials, for example three pearls, six emeralds etc. (using felt-tip pens or collage materials).

● Investigate the symbolism of jewels - and their meanings.

Tudor and Stuart

Elizabethan Accessories

Only wealthy Elizabethans would have owned accessories like these. They were often lavishly embroidered and made from the finest materials. Both men and women wore ruffs which were a sign of wealth and position. A pomander contained aromatic substances to protect against disease and to make the air smell sweet. They were made of silver and gold with jewelled decoration.

Draw and cut out various accessories - hats, gloves, bags, pomander, fan, sword, cap, shoes. Decorate, using any of the above materials. If it is an embroidered article, create the look by drawing patterns on flat tissue with felt-tip pens and then fitting it over the cardboard shape. Lace can be sprayed or decorated with gold paint or pen. Make a ruff by gluing a strip of card on its edge to create folds. To make hats stand out, stuff with tissue paper.

● Make a life-size figure and add all the other accessories. Take a photograph of it, add a frame and make an Elizabethan portrait.

● Look for accessories in portraits of the Elizabethans and make your own versions, e.g. different types of fans, hats, shoes etc.

Materials
Cardboard
Tissue paper - white, red, green
Scraps of lace, ribbons, braid, feathers
Gold paper, gold pen or gold spray
Scraps of foil - blue, red, green, silver, gold
White paper
Felt-tip pens
Scissors and glue

38

Elizabeth I

Elizabeth I loved to wear very elaborate clothes. She wore a stomacher made from whalebone, and a farthingale round her waist to give shape to the heavy skirts. She wore silk stockings and was said to own eighty red wigs. Her sleeves were often the most decorative and valuable part of her wardrobe and were attached with ties. Elizabeth I used preparations to whiten her skin and wore extremely thick make-up. The jewels on her clothes were often symbolic.

Materials

Thin card for figure
Several sheets of white tissue paper
Orange tissue scraps for wig
Lace or doily
Jewellery scraps/pearls
Felt-tip pens in red/grey/yellow/black
Pencils
Scissors and glue

1. Draw a full length figure of Elizabeth in pencil.
2. Spread glue over the lower part of the skirt.
3. Press loosely crumpled large pieces of tissue into the glued area.
4. Cut three layers of tissue to make a skirt.
5. Decorate the top layer with the red, yellow and black felt-tip pens for the jewels and grey for the pattern. Glue the gathered layers together below the waistline.
6. Repeat with three smaller layers to make a frill and glue onto the waistline overlapping the skirt.
7. Cut a piece of cardboard to make a bodice with a long pointed waist. Decorate a piece of tissue with the pattern and glue it over the shape.
8. Cut two identical sleeve shapes. Pad out with pieces of tissue paper and cover with a larger piece of decorated tissue paper. Glue on to the dress.
9. Make a white cloak by gluing lengths of tissue paper along the sides of the figure.
10. If using lace, glue a piece on to a wide strip of white tissue paper and gather along one edge. Glue behind head and attach to the shoulders.
11. Decorate the head using crumpled tissue paper for wig and felt-tip pens for face. Add jewels, sequins and other trimmings.

● This figure can be a freestanding figure (as above) or glued to a background (as on the front cover).

Tudor and Stuart

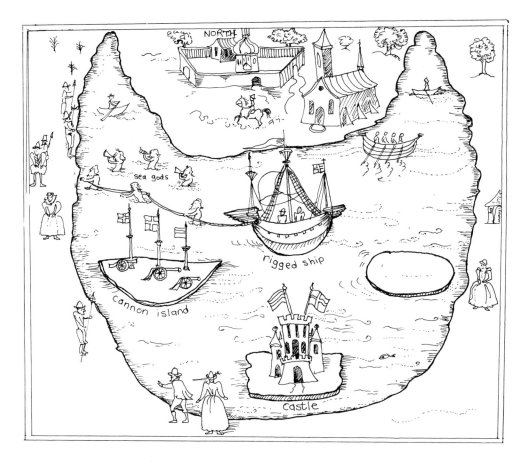

This picture can be photocopied by the teacher, with drawings added by the children

Elizabeth I visited Elvetham, near Aldershot, Surrey, in 1591. Elaborate preparations were made for her visit. A lake was dug out which had floating islands on it. People dressed as sea-gods walked through the water pulling behind them a ship, containing three girls playing cornet music.

● Draw some more islands, with something on each.

● Draw Elizabeth on a throne watching the performance, with courtiers around the lake.

● Draw, or write about, other entertainments you think Elizabeth may have enjoyed.

Drawing of Elizabeth I inspired by a portrait by Marcus Ghaererts

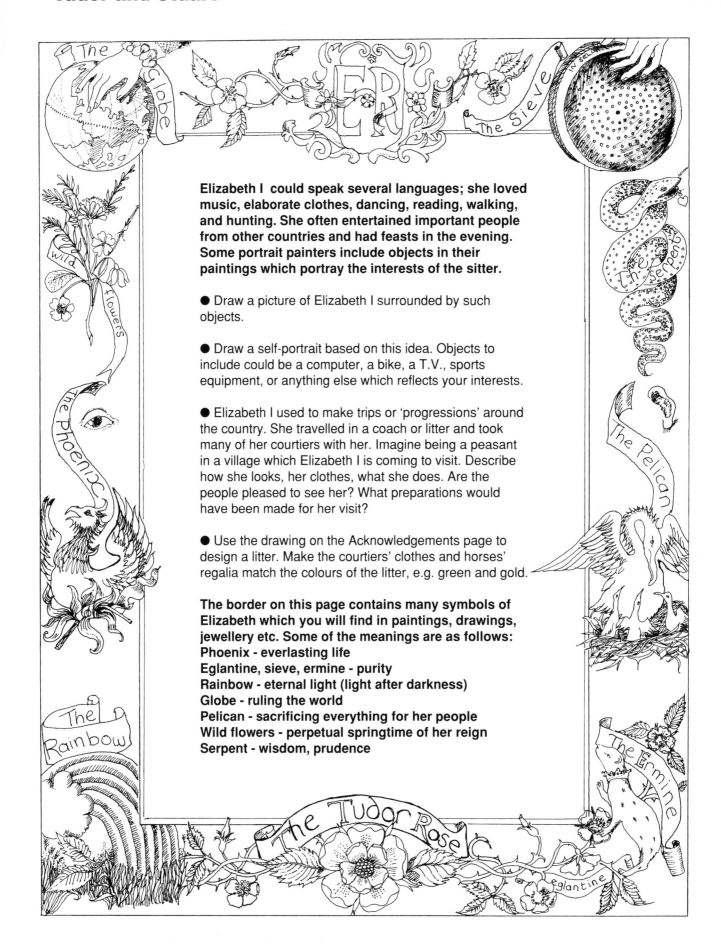

Elizabeth I could speak several languages; she loved music, elaborate clothes, dancing, reading, walking, and hunting. She often entertained important people from other countries and had feasts in the evening. Some portrait painters include objects in their paintings which portray the interests of the sitter.

● Draw a picture of Elizabeth I surrounded by such objects.

● Draw a self-portrait based on this idea. Objects to include could be a computer, a bike, a T.V., sports equipment, or anything else which reflects your interests.

● Elizabeth I used to make trips or 'progressions' around the country. She travelled in a coach or litter and took many of her courtiers with her. Imagine being a peasant in a village which Elizabeth I is coming to visit. Describe how she looks, her clothes, what she does. Are the people pleased to see her? What preparations would have been made for her visit?

● Use the drawing on the Acknowledgements page to design a litter. Make the courtiers' clothes and horses' regalia match the colours of the litter, e.g. green and gold.

The border on this page contains many symbols of Elizabeth which you will find in paintings, drawings, jewellery etc. Some of the meanings are as follows:
Phoenix - everlasting life
Eglantine, sieve, ermine - purity
Rainbow - eternal light (light after darkness)
Globe - ruling the world
Pelican - sacrificing everything for her people
Wild flowers - perpetual springtime of her reign
Serpent - wisdom, prudence

Stuart Family

The Stuarts preferred plain colours compared to the extravagant patterns of the Elizabethans. Falling collars became more popular than ruffs. The child in this picture is a boy even though he is wearing a dress and bonnet. Boys and girls were dressed identically until they were about six years old. This trend continued until Edwardian times.

Draw head and shoulder outlines of a man, woman and child on card and colour the clothes with pastels.

Stuart Boots

Men's boots were made of soft leather in black or pale colours and were not made specifically for right or left feet. They had large turned down cuffs, lavishly lined with lace frills and ruffles. It was fashionable to wear one cuff turned down.

Copy some Stuart boots on to brown paper with felt-tip pens and cut them out. Glue on lace, ribbons, trimmings etc. to decorate the tops of the boots. This makes a good activity for a group of children to make a large board display. Glue them on to a black background with beige strips.

● Try this display idea with hats, gloves or shoes.

● Shoes often had little slots in the sole for hiding letters and secret notes. Write a letter which you would not wish to be discovered by a stranger, and which would be small enough to hide.

Cut out large collars to fit each shape from lace or doily. Draw facial details and hair with felt-tip pens or pastels. Cut out a hat and make a slit across the middle to fit over the top of the head. Glue down and add some feathers. Glue the three figures on to background paper to make a family group.

● Draw a picture of a young boy wearing a dress. Describe how you would feel about this. Was this a good idea? Why would this not happen nowadays?

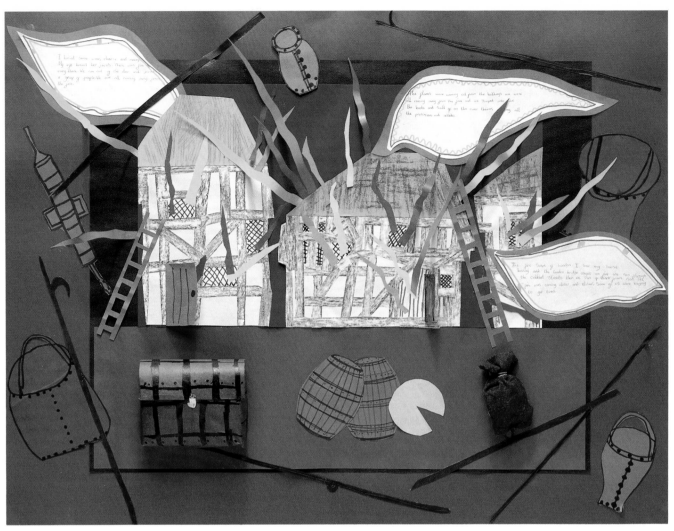

The Great Fire of London

The Great fire of London began in a baker's shop in a street called Pudding Lane. During the fire many people, including the diarist Samuel Pepys, buried personal treasures in their gardens to protect them from damage or theft. Samuel Pepys buried his wine, Parmesan cheese and important documents. For the best eyewitness account of the fire, read Samuel Pepys's diary from 2nd September, l666, onwards.

Materials

Thin card for background
Paper for flames - foil, net, coloured scraps
Narrow strip of card for making beams
Thin paper for rubbing over the strips
Brown wax crayon with paper removed
Cream paper for buildings
Small boxes covered with tissue (for buried treasure)
Brown card for the ground
Felt-tip pens
Scissors and glue

1. Look at pictures of a Tudor street and draw houses on the cream paper.
2. Score long lines on the strip of card with the scissor points.
3. Place thin paper over the strip and rub with the side of a crayon. Repeat several times.
4. Cut these strips out and glue them on to the house shapes to form beams.
5. Use felt-tip pens to draw criss-cross patterns for windows. Glue on doors made from paper scraps.
6. Glue the houses on to the background. Add the lower part of the background.
7. Decorate the 'treasure box' and the other containers and glue on to the background.
8. Cut out flame shapes and glue on to the houses.

● Write about the belongings you would bury to keep safe now, for example, favourite toys, books or anything else which is of value to you.

● Make a list of descriptive 'fire' words. Use the list to write a poem titled 'London's Burning'.

Puritans

Puritans wore plain dark colours without decorations, and their homes and furnishings were very basic. They were sober and serious in their outlook and disapproved of activities such as dancing, sport and music.

Materials
Piece of brown paper for background
White paper for tablecloth, figures and floor
Felt-tip pens or paint, silver pen
Scissors and glue

1. Cut a white piece of paper for the floor and glue it down on the background. Draw lines from a central point to make into tiles.
2. Cut out a white square for the tablecloth and glue part of it over the floor.

3. Using the other white paper, draw two full figures, two half-figures and a baby. Colour in with felt-tip pens or paint in dark colours. Cut out white collars and glue down. Arrange the figures around the table.
4. Make a book from paper and some pewter goblets for the table, using the silver pen.

● Imagine you are a modern-day Puritan. What would you disapprove of? Draw yourself in very plain clothes - and the luxuries you would get rid of.

● Make a miniature book for a Puritan family and write down the rules of the household.

Victorian

Victorian Corner

● Ask throughout the school for contributions of non-valuable artefacts relevant to the period. The costume on the figure is a replica. The corner can be designed around the particular objects brought in.

● Cover the wall with small-patterned wallpaper, attached with adhesive tape. Add strips of dark coloured paper to make a picture rail. Use old nylon curtains and pieces of scrapbox lace to make inner curtains and large window bows. Drape dark coloured material to make the outer curtains.

● Draw around a child lying on a large sheet of paper and transfer the outline to card and cut it out. Dress the figure in a skirt, blouse and shawl. Make a large hat with feathers.

● Cover a small dark wood table with an old-fashioned tablecloth and place appropriate objects on it, for example a quill pen, a silver picture frame, a fan, a pot plant or candlesticks. The Victorians loved a cluttered effect and placed as many objects as possible on shelves or ledges. Mix real objects

with handmade ones. Add a mat or piece of patterned carpet if possible. Make pictures to hang on the wall using oval mounts (see page 47).

● This area could be used for drama activities. Look at life in a rich home at different times of the day. Add more chairs to set the scene.

● Divide the children into groups. Each group acts out one aspect of Victorian home entertainment, e.g. parlour games, poetry reading, musical evening.

● Two children dress up in costume and become the sitters. Children take it in turns to adjust the sitters' positions after deciding who they are and what they are doing. The rest of the other children sketch the final scene. Write a story to go with the picture.

● Practise moving slowly and correctly in the Victorian manner - standing up, sitting down, kneeling (book on head).

Photo Frames

Many Victorian photo frames had an oval mount and an ornate frame. Create a Victorian look by using dull colours, e.g. beige, brown, dark green, wine red.

Materials

Rectangles of paper or card in Victorian colours in two sizes
Oval template of card to fit the smaller rectangle
Rectangles of cream coloured paper for the drawings
Scraps of braid, ribbon and lace
Pencils, felt-tip pens, gold pen

Draw round the oval template, using the smaller rectangle of card or paper. Cut out the oval and glue on to the cream paper. Draw a portrait in the oval. Glue this on to the large rectangle and decorate with scraps of lace and ribbon. Make a hanger from card or ribbon.

Fans

Fans were usually carried in the evening on more formal occasions. It was fashionable to match the colour of the fan with the dress. Fans were made of materials such as of ivory, wood, silk, tortoise-shell, spangles, crêpe or ostrich feathers.

Materials

Pale pink or blue card
White doilies
Scraps of ribbon, jewel trimmings
Silver or gold pen
Pencil
Scissors and strong glue

1. Draw a large feather shape from the card. Cut it out and use as a template to make six more.
2. Spread one feather with strong glue and press pieces of cut-up doily on to it. Repeat for all the feathers.
3. Outline each feather with gold or silver pen.
4. Put some glue on to the base of each feather and press together to form an open fan. Add more glue where necessary to strengthen it.
5. Glue on pieces of decoration and leave to dry.

Victorian

Fruit Dish (Epergne)

The centrepiece of a lavish Victorian banquet was often an elaborate silver or gold dish called an epergne. It contained decorative arrangements of fruit or flowers, built up in a pyramid shape.

Fold a piece of foil in half and draw half a dish as elaborately as possible. Keep folded and cut along the line. Open out and glue on to a dark background. Cut out fruit from gummed paper and glue down in a decorative shape. Use scraps of foil and felt-tip pens to complete the picture.

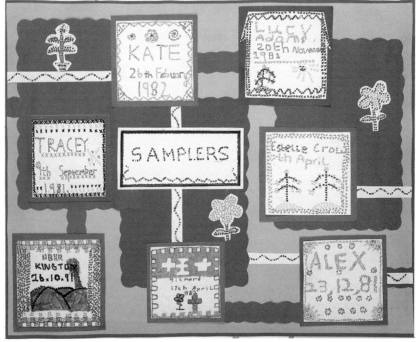

Samplers

Up to 1900 all girls had to sew and embroider a sampler. It was usually made of canvas and stitched with wool in contrasting colours. Using mainly cross-stitch, they copied patterns from books and added their names and date of birth.

Materials
Graph paper
Thin white paper
Adhesive tape
Felt-tip pens

1. Draw a large square on the graph paper with a dark felt-tip pen.
2. Draw a border within the square. Write your first name and date of birth and draw a symmetrical picture of something from nature.
3. Place the thin white paper over the design. Hold it in place with small pieces of adhesive tape rolled between the two sheets, placed outside the square. Follow the pattern using small crosses in brightly coloured pens.

Washstand

Bedrooms in Victorian times always had a 'chamber set', which consisted of a pitcher, or jug, basin, soapdish and powder pot. Bathrooms were only for the very wealthy, and most people had to make do with washing in a basin as there was no running water.

Glue wallpaper on to the upper half of brown background paper. Glue thin strips of brown paper across the wallpaper to give the effect of tiles. Using plain paper, draw and cut out a basin, jug, soapdish and powder pot. Decorate them with flowers cut from wallpaper or wrapping paper, and draw around the flowers with felt-tip pens. Glue a doily on to the washstand and add all the pieces. Complete the picture with felt-tip pens.

Victorian Street

Find or take photographs of a busy modern street. Ask the children to imagine how different the street would have looked in Victorian times. Look at the transport, clothing, shops, roads, lighting, signs. Then discuss Victorian street pictures and compare them with modern ones.

● Make cobblestones on a large sheet of white paper by printing or painting with black paint and finishing off with black felt-tip pens.

● Make lamps from strong black paper and yellow tissue paper. This background can be used to display:-

- Transport pictures printed in black and completed in white paint.
- Drawings of street-sellers, e.g. muffin man, match girl, long song seller (someone who sang and sold topical songs in ballad form), crossing sweep (who swept the dirty roads to make a pathway to protect shoes and clothing).
- Street cries written on scroll shapes and rolled over at the ends.

Change this into a Christmas scene by adding garlands, bows, holly and snow.

49

Victorian

Chimney Sweep

Many Victorian children worked under harsh, cruel conditions in places such as factories and mines. Children also worked as flower-sellers, crossing-sweeps and chimney sweeps. Young boys were often employed as chimney sweeps to climb inside a chimney to brush out the soot. It was dangerous and dirty work and as a result some children died from fallen soot while trapped inside the chimney.

Materials
Dull coloured paper for background
Brown cardboard for the figure
Black tissue paper
Grey paper, crumpled then opened out
Charcoal or black crayon
White chalk
Felt-tip pens
Scissors and glue

Draw and cut out a figure of a chimney sweep. Make clothes using crumpled, torn paper and black tissue paper. Decorate with patches and smudged charcoal and crayon. Glue the figure on to a background and add details in white chalk.

● Make pictures in the same way of other working children, e.g. matchgirl, flower-seller, factory worker, mud-lark.

Inn Signs

Make a symmetrical shape by folding a piece of paper in half and cutting a pattern at the top. Open out and use as a template to make an inn sign from a piece of card. Design and write the name based on a Victorian theme, e.g. Penny Farthing, Queen Victoria, Hansom Cab, Prince Albert. Use felt-tip pens to draw an appropriate picture. Outline the sign with black and gold. Use black paper to make a bracket for hanging the sign.

Christmas Tree Decorations

Most of our modern Christmas customs are based on traditions which originated in Victorian times, e.g. greeting cards, crackers, room and tree decorations. A recent commercial revival in Victoriana has made it easy to obtain reproduction decorations. These provide a good source of inspiration for art ideas.

Make a Victorian Christmas display using either a small tree or a branch set in a pot. Trim the tree with Victorian decorations. Drape an area with red cloth and decorate with a selection of natural objects such as pine cones, holly, evergreens and other berries.

Drum
Cut a small card tube into thirds. Cut two circles of white paper larger than the ends of the tube. Make cuts around the edge of the circle and glue down on to the tube. Cover the tube with a strip of dark green paper. Decorate with strips of red paper and gold thread. Add drumsticks made from matches and red Plasticine. Glue on a loop of ribbon to make a hanger. (Double-sided adhesive tape is very useful for adding decoration.)

Scroll
Cut a rectangle of dull pink paper. Serrate the edges. Roll the top and bottom in opposite directions and glue down. Decorate with miniature music and picture scraps (see pages 69 and 70). Make a hanger from gold thread.

Music Book
Cut a rectangle of card. Cut a piece of coloured paper larger than the cardboard shape. Fold and glue down the edges. Glue on a piece of miniature music to fit the book. Add ribbon and other small decorations.

Soldier
Cut a strip of card. Cover both sides with strips of red and blue. Draw and cut out the shape of a soldier and glue on a face using white paper. Add details in felt-tip pens.

Other decorations suitable for a Victorian tree are:- trumpets, flags, fans, candy canes, hearts, dolls, boxes, tartan bows, pincushions, swords, fruit decorated with gold, bouquet holders, tambourines and fiddles. Most of these could be made two-dimensionally in card decorated with scraps.

Victorian

Crackers

Crackers were first made in England by Tom Smith who was a sweet maker. He copied the French idea of decorating sweets to increase the sales. He added a snap, and crackers became a Christmas tradition.

Roll up a piece of thin cardboard to make a thin tube. Secure with adhesive tape. Fringe the ends of three layers of tissue (twice the width of the cardboard) and roll these round the tube. Glue down. Twist the ends of the crackers and tie with ribbon. Use gold paper to decorate and add tissue paper flowers and other decorations.

● Decorate a box and fill it with pairs of identical crackers with sweets and a joke inside them.

● Make miniature crackers to decorate a card.

Pen Wiper

Victorians valued handmade gifts very highly, particularly those made by children. One favourite was the hand-shaped pen wiper originally made from white card and black velvet. The motto was stitched with beads.

Materials
White card
Black felt-tip pen
Black paper
Lace
Ribbon
White pencil or paint and thin brush

Draw round your hand on the white card. Cut this out and turn it over. Use a black felt-tip pen to draw the stitches. Glue on a piece of black paper and lace. Tie a dark coloured ribbon round the wrist. Add a motto in white pencil or paint, e.g. Many hands make light work.

● Make miniature pen wipers to hang on a Christmas tree.

● Make a classroom list of sayings and mottoes.

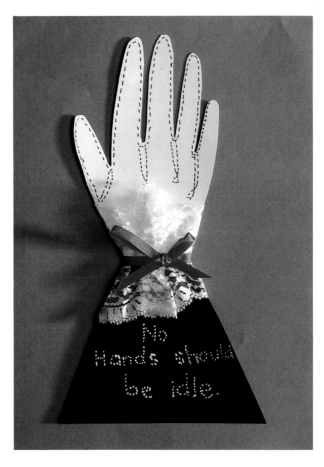

Christmas Cards

The first Christmas card appeared in 1843. It was commissioned by Sir Henry Cole for family and friends. The card was coloured by hand and one thousand were printed. The idea of Christmas cards grew in popularity. Early cards featured violets, ferns, ivy, robins and holly. The Victorians designed cards in the shape of ovals, crescents, diamonds, bells and circles, and folded them in interesting ways.

See the photographs above for examples of card shapes.

Materials

Cream and pastel coloured paper and card
Photo-copied pictures which are suitable: scraps (see page 69), motifs from reproduction cards
Scraps of lace, doily, ribbon
Felt-tip pens in purple, green, red, pink, gold and silver
Scissors and glue

Fold the card or stiff paper and cut into a variety of shapes. Decorate with violets, ivy, ferns etc. Add scraps of lace, doily, ribbon. Complete with gold or silver pen. Find some suitable Christmas messages.

Victorian

The Toy Box

Toys were either home-made or bought from toy shops and bazaars. Many of these were miniatures of objects in the outside world, e.g. soldiers and forts, drums, yachts, engines and tea-sets. Some other toys were hobby horses, building blocks, jack-in-a-box and kites. Favourite games were skittles, marbles and playing cards. Many families had a strong decorated wooden box to store the toys.

All the toys listed above can be made from card, paper, scraps and felt-tip pens. To make the toy box, choose a dull colour card, e.g. dark green or wine red. Make two rectangles, one smaller than the other. Fold down the upper edge of the large rectangle. Lay out both the rectangles on a background. Arrange the toys in the box and glue the box and the toys down. Decorate the box with gold pen and scraps of gold paper. This makes an ideal large board display.

Crinoline Doll

A crinoline was a metal or whalebone cage worn under a wide gathered skirt. It replaced the fashion for wearing lots of petticoats to support the skirt. Women enjoyed a new freedom of movement. However, the huge billowing skirts had some disadvantages, such as knocking over furniture and catching fire.

Materials
Cardboard for figure
Tissue paper in a variety of colours
Lace, sequins, ribbon trimmings
Felt-tip pens
Adhesive tape (double-sided, if possible)
Scissors and glue

1. Draw and cut out a figure from cardboard and draw the face.
2. Cover the bodice with tissue paper glued on to the front and back, and decorate.
3. Make a very full skirt by gluing frills and lace to the bottom of a double strip of tissue. Gather the skirt on to a piece of adhesive tape to fit the waist of the doll.
4. Design and make a bonnet and fan.
5. To make the figure stand up, stuff the skirt with tissue paper.

● Dress dolls in a variety of fashions of the Victorian era.

Jigsaw Puzzle

Materials
Square of thin card for jigsaw in beige colour
Coloured card for the background in dark red, green or brown
Felt-tip pen, ruler, circle template
Scissors and glue
A book with Victorian pictures, e.g. Punch and Judy, rocking horse

1. With felt-tip pen, draw round the circle template on the thin beige card. Copy the Victorian picture inside.
2. Draw a floral border round the edge.
3. Draw along both sides of a ruler to form a grid across the picture.
4. Photocopy the child's picture as a reference to help assemble the jigsaw.
5. Cut the picture along the lines of the grid.
6. The pieces can be kept separately and used as a jigsaw or glued on to a background.

● For younger children make a very large grid with just four or six pieces to assemble. Use a simplified outline.

Spoon Dolls

Poor people could not afford to buy toys so they made their own. Dolls were made from wooden spoons and rags. Many children created home-made versions of manufactured toys such as hoops, cup and ball sets, and bats.

Material
1 wooden spoon
Strong card
Pieces of material, ribbon, wool
Felt-tip pens, pencil
Scissors and strong glue

1. Place the wooden spoon on the card and draw round it with a pencil, or use the wooden spoon to make the doll.
2. Cut this out and draw a face on it with felt-tip pens.
3. Place a piece of fabric round the stick and wind the wool round this to make a waist. Add more pieces of fabric if needed to make cloaks and belts.
4. Spread glue on the head and add pieces of fabric cut into headscarves and shawls.

● Make other toys using only scraps of material, pieces of wood and odds and ends.

● Make a doll using an old-fashioned wooden peg or a modern wooden one.

Victorian

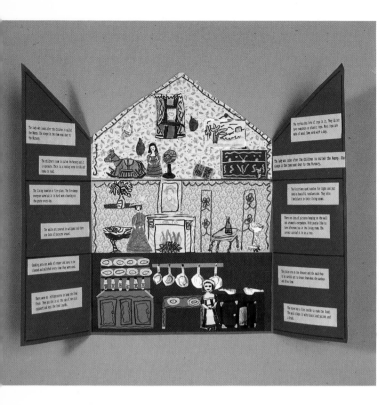

Doll's House

Dolls' houses were exact in many details, and contained exact miniatures of real things.

Materials
Piece of card in dark red, green or brown
Piece of white or cream paper
Scraps of coloured paper, fabric and wallpaper
Felt-tip pens
Scissors and glue

1. Talk about the things you would find in a Victorian kitchen, living room and nursery.
2. Fold the edges of the card in to the middle and cut a pointed roof shape.
3. Glue down two different strips of wallpaper to form the two upper levels of the house.
4. Decorate each level with furniture made from scraps.

Level one - Kitchen - open range, dresser with crockery, table, chairs.
Level two - Living room - dark-wood furniture, red curtains, pictures on wall.
Level three - Nursery - rocking horse, cradle, toy box, toy pram.

5. Draw the doors and windows on the front of the house and decorate with felt-tip pens.

Jack-in-a-Box

Two square pieces of paper in beige, red, dark green or brown
Strip of paper in any of the above colours
Piece of paper for the head and hat
Scraps of coloured paper
Gold pen
Felt-tip pens
Scissors and glue

1. Cut one square of paper smaller than the other and glue down.
2. Fan fold the strip and glue one end at the back of the square.
3. Cut out a face and hat, and glue on to the other end of the strip. Add a fan-folded collar.
4. Use coloured scraps to make eyes and mouth and decorations for the hat.
5. Add other details in gold pen.

● Make up a simple class poem or story about a Jack-in-a-box.

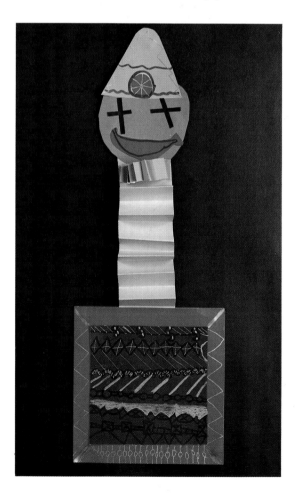

Models and Toys

Toy Fort
Paint the lid of a shoebox grey to make the base. Make cuts at regular intervals around the rim of the lid. Bend down alternate pieces and then cut them off. Use this technique to make the top of the towers. Fold two identical pieces of cardboard to form square towers. Paint these grey, and when dry glue on to the base. Draw stones with black felt-tip pen. Add sentry boxes made from cardboard rolls. Paint some clothes pegs red and black to make soldiers. Add hats, arms and weapons using coloured pipe cleaners.

Box of Toys
Many Victorian toys were bought and kept in small wooden boxes. Paint a divided box and lid with thick brown paint all over. Children can design and make their own version of small Victorian toys, e.g. cup and ball, yo-yo, marbles, dominoes, jacks.

Punch and Judy
Punch and Judy shows were enjoyed by many Victorians at the seaside. Find pictures of these and compare with modern ones. Using a rectangular box, cut out a window in the top third. Paint the box with thick red paint. When dry, glue on white paper strips. Paint the inside of the box black and glue on curtains. Make simple puppets from card and felt-tip pens. Write a script for a Punch and Judy show. A full size version can be made with papier mâché puppets.

Screen
Victorian bedrooms often had a wooden screen which was beautifully decorated with picture scraps. The screen provided an area for dressing and undressing.

Materials
Large sheet of black cardboard
Small Victorian scraps (replicas, see page 69), or pictures from magazines, or pieces from Victorian style wrapping paper and greeting cards
Paper for mounting small pictures and making the border
Thin paint wash in light brown (or use a tea bag)
Pencils
Scissors and glue

1. Fold the black card into six equal parts. Draw a line with a pencil to make a border all round the edge.
2. Cut out the small pictures. Photocopy if there are not enough to cover the screen. Colour black and white pictures with pencils. Wash over the pictures to give antique look.
3. Glue them on to the mounting paper and cut around, leaving an edge. Glue these on to the screen, leaving the border. Add strips of paper along the edges.

Victorian

Sailing Ship

Clippers were triple-masted sailing ships and faster than most steamers of the time. The most famous of these graceful ships was the _Cutty Sark_, which originally carried tea and later transported wool from Australia.

Materials

Sheet of white paper or thin card for the background
A piece of blue tissue paper, larger than the background
A piece of white paper for sails and boat
Scissors and glue

1. Place the sheet of background paper on top of the blue tissue paper. Glue down the excess tissue paper at the back. Turn the paper over.
2. Draw and cut out the hull of a sailing ship, using the white paper, and glue down. Cut out shapes to make the sails. Fold the edges of each sail back and glue on to the masts, making the sails stand out.
3. Add details, using white paper, e.g. ropes, small sails, flags etc. Try this as a black silhouette on coloured tissue or a white background. Design a frame with a nautical theme, e.g. rope design, anchors, life-belts etc.

Servants

Materials

Coloured paper for background
Thin card for figure
Tissue paper in black and white
White doily and silver foil for parlour maid
Felt-tip pen
Scissors and glue

1. Draw a figure on the card.
2. Cut out a black bodice and glue down. Make a skirt by gathering a rectangle of black tissue at one edge. Glue it on to the waist and along each side.
3. Make the skirt stand out by crushing up tissue and placing it underneath.
4. Glue on an apron made from white tissue.
5. If it is a parlour maid add white doily to the cap and apron and a silver tray made from foil.

Servant's Corner

In Victorian times, servants were very often poorly paid, so middle class families could afford at least one servant called 'the maid of all work'. Wealthier families had many servants who worked long hours with very little time off. The housekeeper was responsible for all the servants and the running of the household. The 'tweenie', or between stairs maid, was very often a girl of eleven or twelve years of age. She had the worst jobs to do, such as washing greasy pans and scrubbing floors.

Collect as many old-fashioned artefacts as possible from children. If this is not possible, make cardboard cut-outs of objects, e.g. washboard, carpet beater, iron etc. Paint them in suitable colours and add texture, e.g. corrugated card for washboard. Hang a white sheet up for the background and pin a washing line across it. Use *old* wooden pegs (i.e. two-prong, not wire clip) to hang white washing along the line. Make clothes from white paper and doilies if there are no suitable real clothes. Use some lace cloths or doilies to decorate the area. Display objects in suitable places - on a table, in

baskets or in pottery dishes. Add pot-pourri and bunches of dried herbs and lavender. Creative writing can be displayed with pictures from calendars, magazines and books.Servants would have used some of the following in their daily routines:

Laundry - dolly pegs, washboard, clothes pegs, irons, mangle, washing tub, starch, blue bag, wooden tongs, wooden stirring stick.
Kitchen - butter pats, poker, toasting fork, broom, bowls, jelly moulds, whisk, pestle and mortar, bread board, rolling pin, wooden sieve and pastry brush.
Cleaning - housemaid's box: a wooden box containing such items as brushes, dusters, cloths and a polish for black-leading the stove.

● Compare modern day jobs with those from the last century. List the jobs you don't like doing. Set up a modern ironing/cleaning corner next to a Victorian one. Use for drama activities - 'then and now'. Dress up several children in costume. Ask each group to explain to the others about life in their time.

Victorian

Victorian Books

In Victorian times, at last, children had books written just for them. There were fairy stories from Europe - the Brothers Grimm and Hans Anderson; fantasy books such as *Alice in Wonderland* and *Peter Pan* and adventure tales such as *Treasure Island* and *The Swiss Family Robinson*. These books are still popular today. Improved methods of printing made the books more enjoyable by including beautiful drawings, some in colour. Children were entertained by pop-up books and movable illustrations while the stories were supposed to teach them to be good.

Find pictures of nursery rhyme characters and write the rhyme on a scroll, miniature book or decorated shape. Make bookmarks from picture scraps, lace and ribbons. Make a zig-zag alphabet and small books.

● Choose a book title and make a corner in the classroom which brings the story to life, e.g. *Treasure Island* . Create a Victorian look by using appropriate colours and copying Victorian illustrations. Act out the story.

● Experiment with movable and pop-up pictures to incorporate in a book.

Twentieth Century

At The Seaside

This series was designed for a hall or corridor. However, most of the ideas can be used separately in the classroom. The work on the l900's was done by older children and the l990's by the youngest age group.

The seaside is an ideal theme because so many photographs have been taken there by parents and grandparents. Other themes which could work well, spread across the decades, are:-

Toys - a shop window, a toy box or a child's room
Transport - Going on a trip
Parties - Christmas party, birthday party
School - Inside or outside

Pictures can be placed anywhere on the backgrounds to create a montage. Real objects, e.g. record covers, clothing, photographs, can be mixed with the artwork. Children can get ideas from historical packs, books, song-sheets etc.

1900's

Walking along the promenade was a popular seaside activity. At the end of the 19th Century children did not swim, but paddled almost fully clothed. After 1900, people began to wear bathing costumes which they wore on the beach and therefore enjoyed more freedom.

For the banner or awning make a template by fan-folding a long strip of white paper. Cut a curve at one end and open out. Draw around this on red paper or card. Cut the white strip into separate sections and glue down alternately to make red and white stripes.

Victorian/Edwardian figures - Make these from tissue and paper.
Scrap albums - Use reproduction scraps or the ideas at the back of the book (pages 69 and 70)

Postcard albums - Postcards, as they are now, appeared in 1902 when the Post Office allowed the sending of a picture card with a written message. Postcards were avidly collected and pasted in special albums. Photocopy old postcards or draw old-fashioned scenes, and colour them with pencils or thin paints. Copy or make up your own messages for the other side. Cut narrow strips of the background colour and glue them diagonally across the postcard corners.
Songsheets - Find some old seaside songs. Copy the songs by hand on to manuscript paper and decorate around the edges with felt-tip pens.
Flags - Make by decorating triangles of coloured paper with pictures in felt-tip pen. Staple them together at the corners to form a row of flags.
Other details - Add bathing suits, sailor suits, bathing machines, hot air balloons.

Twentieth Century

1930's

At this time men were still wearing one-piece costumes which had low necks and backs and were much shorter. Most costumes were made of machine knitted wool. Women's costumes were one-piece or two-piece and were sometimes cut away at the back. Children also wore one-piece costumes and sun bonnets. Bathing caps were made of rubber and were usually white. Rubber bathing shoes were worn by all ages.

Sea-shell ornaments
Glue shells on to card to make a figure or creature, using strong glue. Cut around them and add details with marker pens.

Picture frames from sea-shells
Cut an oval or round-shaped frame from silver card. Glue the frame on to blue paper. Draw figures in l930's beachwear (note the fashion for white belts).

Trim around the frame and decorate by gluing down shells.

Towels - Make the fashionable 'rising sun' motif using orange-red and yellow paper on black. These towels were sometimes used as a 'wrap' or became a cloak or screen for dressing and undressing.

Other details - Add Punch and Judy show, ice-cream cart, aeroplane etc. Find out about traditional beach entertainment. When did it start? Some, such as Punch and Judy shows, would be used for many years and enjoyed by several generations of children from mid-Victorian times onwards. Photographs taken through the decades show very little change in the booths and puppet show.

1960's

Photo album - Photocopy black and white beach pictures of the period. Glue on to black paper. Glue small black triangles on the corners to look like photo mounts. Which music was popular (e.g. The Beach Boys)? Look at pictures, books of l960's fashion - bikinis, sunglasses, beehive hairdos etc.

Bathing hats - Draw and cut out a round shape from coloured paper. Glue on flower shapes. Make a face to fit the hat and glue down.

Beach bag - Decorate a piece of tissue paper with felt-tip pens. Glue down to form a bag shape on the background and stuff with more tissue paper. Add a strip of paper for handle.

Ice-cream sundaes - Draw sundae dish shapes from white paper. Cut out ice-cream from coloured tissue paper.

Ask parents and grandparents to write about their memories of a day at the seaside in the 1960's. What did they do? What did they wear? What did they have to eat? Would they buy food on the beach? How did they get there? How long did they stay? Where did they stay? Talk about games, entertainment, water sports, toys and equipment, changing into swimwear, sun protection.

1990's

Sunglasses - Cut sunglasses frames from card to fit the individual child. Cut out the centre from each lens and cover with Cellophane paper. Add 'legs' to fit round the ears.

Swimsuit pictures - Cut a wavy strip from card. Place under a thin piece of paper and rub with the side of a crayon. Move the strip around and rub several times to make the water. Draw figures wearing swimsuits on this background, using felt-tip pens. Colour with a crayon. Add further details, e.g. beach towels, beach balls.

T-shirts and short sets - Draw and cut out a white T-shirt from paper. Glue on to a piece of coloured paper to fit the bottom of the T-shirt. Cut out a 'V' shape from the coloured paper to make shorts. Decorate the T-shirt with felt-tip pens.

● Discuss how in recent times there has been an awareness of skin damage by the sun. Make bottles of sun cream with numbers showing the degree of protection from the sun. Talk about other ways of protecting the skin, e.g. hats and umbrellas, and use these in the poster.

● Add a clock to show the most dangerous exposure times to the sun.

● Design a 'Save your skin' poster. Cut pictures out of magazines showing suncreams, hats, umbrellas and use these in the poster.

● Make a list of words connected with skincare, e.g. ozone layer, ultra-violet rays, protection factor etc.

● Create a beach-front shop with collections of clothes, buckets and spades, souvenirs, swimwear, towels, skin cream, rugs, pictures of ice cream and drinks, beach chair, toys etc.

1960's Corner

All objects in this photograph were collected by a group of children. Items to collect could include: record covers, wigs, platform sole shoes, mini-dresses, long strings of beads, belts, flared trousers, headbands, photographs, ties.

This group had a dress-up 1960's day and danced to the music of the period, e.g. jiving and rock'n'rolling, taught by some of the parents. Photographs of this era are included in the display. A few objects from another era, e.g. 1930's, 1950's, could be added to the main display: spot the odd ones out!

To make the 'hippy'

Draw around a child on paper. Use this as a template and cut out the figure from card. If the card is not big enough, add a separate head from another sheet of card. Paint the head, arms and feet, and dress the figure in 'hippy' clothes - flowery patterns, loose jacket, flared trousers, beads and headband. The 'flares' for this figure were made by slashing the sides of a modern pair of jeans and inserting a triangle of patterned fabric. The figure was suspended from the ceiling on a string covered with tissue flowers. The 'hippy' could also be made to stand upright on a stick and block of wood. Many old record covers have good ideas for display and lettering. Small 45's can be made from black cardboard and the names of popular songs printed on them. When the area is set up, some parents might like to come in and chat about fashions, interests, cars etc.

● Collect photographs of parents and grandparents in the 1960's. Display on a 'psychedelic' background. Can you guess whose relatives are in the photographs?

Twentieth Century

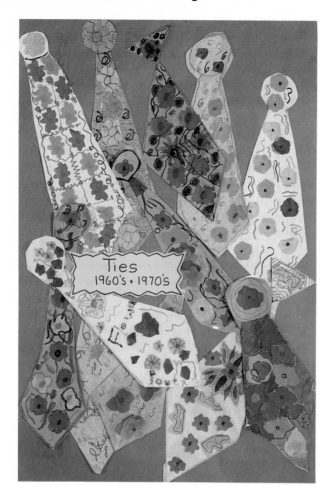

1960's and 1970's Ties

Men's ties were often very wide and brightly patterned in the late 1960's and early 1970's. If possible, look at some real ties from this era. Draw some of the designs on paper first.

Materials
Long rectangles of white paper
Pastel coloured tissue paper, larger than the tie
A variety of tissue paper scraps
Felt-tip pens, pencil
Scissors and glue

With a pencil, draw the tie with a knot at the top, and cut this out. Place this on the tissue paper and draw around the tie shape, leaving a wide edge to overlap on the back. Glue along the edges of the white tie and fold the surplus tissue on to the glue. Turn the tie over and draw a design on the tie with felt-tip pens, adding tissue paper shapes.

● Make a flowery shirt front and place the tie on it. Make it into a 'gift set'.

● Add a neck strip so the tie can be worn.

● Make a display with a giant-size tie. Add writing and flowery ties.

Headbands

In the 1960's, long straight hair was fashionable. 'Hippies' often wore a woven band with feathers, and they wore flowers in their hair. 'Flower Power' started in America, in San Francisco, and spread to other countries.

Materials
Cardboard strips long enough to make a headband
Scraps of tissue paper and gummed paper
Gold or silver thread (or wool)
Felt-tip pens, adhesive tape
Scissors and glue

Decorate the headband with flowers made from tissue paper. On the inside, tape different lengths of thread and attach flowers and feathers in the threads.

Posters

This is a quick way to display visual information about an era. Children choose a subject, e.g. fashion, news headlines, pop-stars, games, books, advertisements. Collect old magazines and newspapers and photocopy these. They can be reduced or enlarged to make a more interesting display.

Souvenirs

Make a collection of modern souvenirs which have some historic decoration, e.g. T-shirts, mugs, rulers, pencils, tea towels, pennants, bookmarks, tea-cosies, oven gloves etc.

Design your own historical souvenir on card or paper using paints or felt-tip pens, e.g. cut out a T-shirt shape, add a drawing and an appropriate caption.

● Display these designs to look like a shop window, e.g. stacked cup designs, pennants hung behind, etc.

Record Covers

● Find some colourful 1960's record covers and make your own version using felt-tip pens on coloured card. Make up your own titles for them, and try a variety of lettering.

● Make a list of song categories, e.g. pop, instrumental, rock'n'roll, folk, rhythm and blues, soul etc. Look at the Top 20 now and classify the songs.

● Look at the names of pop groups from the period, e.g. The Searchers, The Fortunes, Herman's Hermits, The Rocking Berries, The Yardbirds.

● Invent your own 1960's group. Design the costumes and musical instruments. Create a name for the group and think of ways to advertise it.

● Mime to 1960's records. Look at the clothing and hairstyles of various groups and compare them with those of today.

● Find out the prices of the different records of the 1960's, e.g. LP's - 12 tracks, 6 on each side
    EP's - 4 tracks, 2 on each side
    45's (singles) - 1 track
(The speed was altered for each type of record.)

● About six 45's could be stacked on a record player, which automatically dropped them one at a time on to the turntable. Ask adults to help you make a list of words and expressions from the 1960's which are no longer in use, e.g. swinging party, fab, 'peace man', dolly bird, mod, gear, flares, beehive hairdos, a good beat, hits and misses (records).

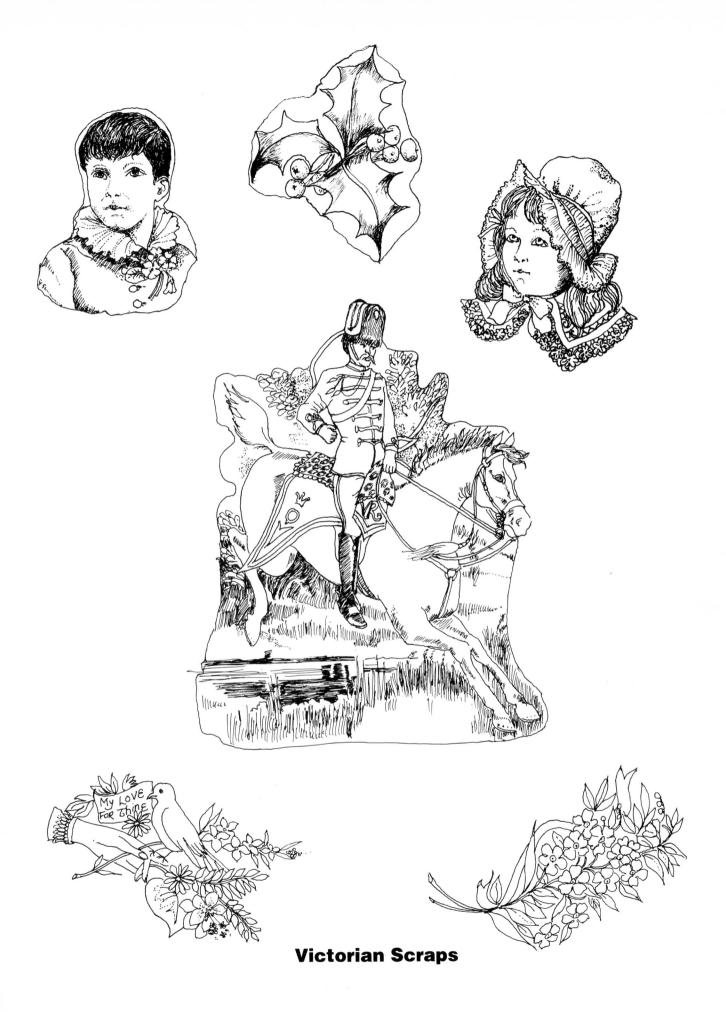

Victorian Scraps

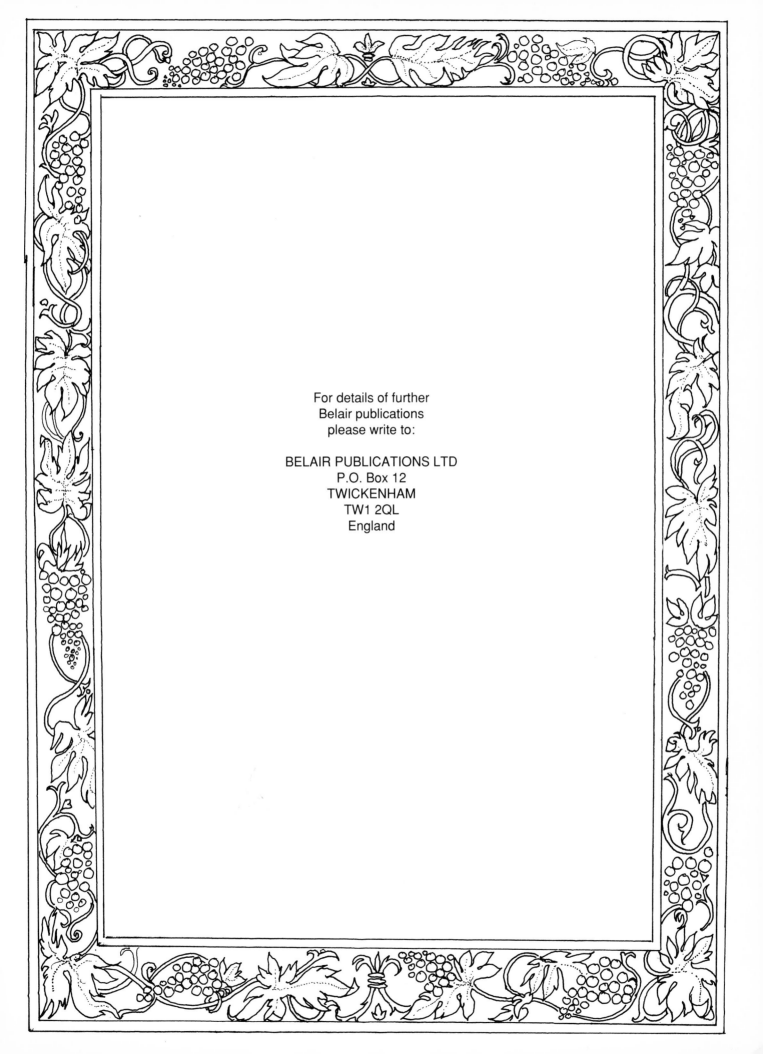

For details of further
Belair publications
please write to:

BELAIR PUBLICATIONS LTD
P.O. Box 12
TWICKENHAM
TW1 2QL
England

Notes